Nita Mehta
SANDWICHES
TOASTED PLAIN GRILLED

Nita Mehta

B.Sc. (Home Science), M.Sc. (Food and Nutrition), Gold Medalist

Coauthor

MEENAKSHI AHUJA

SNAB
Publishers Pvt Ltd

Nita Mehta's
S ANDWICHE S
TOASTED PLAIN GRILLED

© Copyright 1997-2002 **SNAB** Publishers Pvt Ltd

5th Print 2002
ISBN 81-86004-21-1

Food Styling and Photography: **SNAB**

Layout and laser typesetting :

 National Information Technology Academy
3A/3, Asaf Ali Road
New Delhi-110002
N.I.T.A.
☎ 3252948

Published by :

SNAB
Publishers Pvt. Ltd.
3A/3 Asaf Ali Road,
New Delhi - 110002
Tel: 3252948, 3250091
Telefax:91-11-3250091

Editorial and Marketing office:
E-348, Greater Kailash-II, N.Delhi-48
Fax: 91-11-6235218 *Tel:* 91-11-6214011, 6238727
E-Mail: nitamehta@email.com
snab@snabindia.com
Website: http://www.nitamehta.com
Website: http://www.snabindia.com

Distributed by :

THE VARIETY BOOK DEPOT
A.V.G. Bhavan, M 3 Con Circus,
New Delhi - 110 001
Tel : 3327175, 3322567; Fax : 3714335

Printed by :

THOMSON PRESS (INDIA) LIMITED

Rs. 89/-

Contents

A good cup of tea   12
A good cup of instant coffee   13
Frothy espresso coffee   14
VEGETARIAN SANDWICHES   15
    Open Pasta Sandwich   16
    Spicy Beans with Cottage Cheese   20
    Grilled Cheese & Vegetable Sandwich   22
    Toasted Club Sandwich   23
    Mushroom Triangles   24
    Cottage Cheese Sandwich   25
    Apple & Cheese Sandwiches   26
    Macaroni Open Sandwich   27
    Sandwich Faces   28
    Corn & Mushroom Toasts   30

Brown Vegetable Sandwich 31
Vegetable Burgers with Cole Slaw 32
Cream-Curd Surprise 34
Sandwiched Peas 37
Rainbow Sandwich 38
Cheese-Raisin Sandwich 39
Jumbo Sandwich 40
Corn Footlongs 42
Swiss Circles 44
Yoghurt Toasts 46
Teen Burgers 47
Moong Toast 48
East-West Sandwich 50
Party Sandwich 51
Curd Vegetable Fingers 56
Grilled Chilli Cheese Sandwich 58

NON-VEGETARIAN SANDWICHES   59

Ham-Tomato Sandwich   60

Chicken Burgers   61

Cheese & Luncheon Meat Fingers   62

Mock Pizza   63

Yoghurt Prawn Sandwich   64

Sandwich Loaf   65

Devilled Ham Sandwich   66

Salami Sandwich   67

Bacon Burgers   68

Double Decker   70

Devil's Delight   74

Chicken Hawaii   75

Tuna Sandwiches   76

Sandwiches with Chicken Left over   77

Shrimp Sandwiches   78

Pyramid Sandwiches 79
Egg Cheese Toast 80
Junglee Sandwiches 81
Baked Ham & Tomato Sandwiches 82
Tomato Egg Toasts 84
Sausages in Jackets 85
Egg Quickie 86
Fried Cheese Sandwich 87
Cheese & Bacon Rolls 88
Tricoloured Sandwich 89

BASIC RECIPES 92
Thousand Island Dressing 92
Poodina (Mint) Chutney 92
White Sauce 93
Mayonnaise 94, 95

Tips about Sandwiches

- Relish toasted and grilled sandwiches for breakfast. These may be cut into smaller pieces for an evening snack. Toast & grill the slices patiently till golden brown and crisp, to really enjoy it with the filling.
- To grill sandwiches, remove all metal plates from the oven, except the wire grill. Preheat oven to maximum temperature with the top & bottom heating rods 'ON'. Butter the sandwich on the outer side also (both sides) with softened butter & place on the wire grill or wire rack for 2-3 min.
- In winters toasted, grilled or pan sauted sandwiches taste better. Use leftover breads for this, as it restores freshness.
- Use different breads for variety - brown bread, spice bread, milk bread, as well as buns or rolls for a wider selection of sandwiches.
- Keep a bottle of ready made mayonnaise in the fridge. It turns out to be very handy. Mayonnaise is easily available in all stores and even at the bakeries.
- Replace the heel or crust end on the loaf to avoid drying out of bread.

- Soften butter or margarine for easy, economical spreading.
- Spread softened butter or margarine to edges of bread slices. Softened butter, margarine, cream cheese or peanut butter will form a protective coating, preventing moist fillings from soaking into the bread.
- Avoid **melted** butter or margarine, as they will **soak** into the bread and make a soggy sandwich. Moist salad dressings if spread directly onto bread will have a similar effect. Use latter only after the slices are spread with the softened butter or margarine.
- Avoid having too much filling or topping - it makes the sandwich untidy.
- If the filling contains too much moisture, apply it just before serving or lay a lettuce leaf on the buttered bread before applying the filling.
- 500 gm softened butter will spread 80 slices if 1 tsp is used per slice.
- Wrap sandwiches without cutting the sides, in foil or in a damp napkin to keep them supple and fresh. Cut the crust only at the time of serving to prevent the edges from drying.
- Use a sharp knife preferably with a saw edge and dip occasionally in hot water for cutting sandwiches. Cut sandwiches into interesting shapes.

Gay Garnishes

Colourful garnishes add a touch of sophistication to sandwiches. Match sticks of carrot and fine strips of lettuce or cabbage lend colour. A sprig of mint or parsley along with a few potato chips makes a serving of toasted sandwiches more appetizing. Open sandwiches may also be garnished with finely grated processed cheese or paneer. Cole slaw, pickled onion or cucumber & French fries may accompany toasted or grilled sandwiches.

Slices of tomato or cucumber should be overlapped when placed between two slices of bread, while making sandwiches. This way they show more when the sandwich is cut. Cucumber should not be peeled, as the peel adds colour, but remember to choose a fresh and tender cucumber. A palak (spinach) leaf blanched by dipping in boiling water for a few seconds and then refreshed in cold water may be put between a tomato sandwich. This green leaf being darker in colour than lettuce looks more interesting than a lettuce or a cabbage green. Remember to place some of the sandwiches upright in the serving platter, so that the filling shows. For that, cut the sandwiches into 3-4 pieces as shown on pages 10-11. The rest I leave to your imagination........

Nita Mehta

Ideas for Cutting of Sandwiches

MORE Ideas for Cutting of Sandwiches

A good cup of tea

with sandwiches makes them more tasty!

<u>Serving 2 cups</u>

2 cups water
1 tsp ordinary tea leaves (Red label)
1½ tsp long, flavoured tea leaves (Lipton Green label tea)
¼ cup milk, sugar to taste

1. Put water to boil in a pan or degchi.
2. Just as it is **about** to boil, add ordinary tea leaves.
3. Reduce flame as soon as it boils. Add flavoured, long tea leaves. Stir.
4. Wait for a few seconds, **but do not let the tea boil.**
5. Just when it is about to boil, add milk.
6. Keeping the flame low, when the tea is **just about to boil**, remove from fire and strain into cups which have been rinsed with hot water.

A good cup of instant hot coffee

1½ cups water
½ cup milk
2½ tsp instant coffee powder (Nescafe)
2 tsp sugar or to taste

1. Strain milk in a pan or degchi. Add water.
2. Keep on fire to boil.
3. Put 1¼ tsp coffee powder and 1 tsp sugar in each cup.
4. When the milk-water mixture boils, reduce flame and simmer for a minute.
5. Remove from fire and pour into cups from a little height to get a frothy coffee. Stir and serve immediately.

Frothy espresso coffee

<u>Serving 2 cups</u>

1½ cups water
½ cup milk
3 tsp instant coffee powder (Nescafe)
3 tsp sugar or to taste
a little drinking chocolate to sprinkle - optional

1. Beat sugar and coffee powder vigorously in an old tea cup with a spoon till light and fluffy, adding few drops of water to facilitate beating.
2. Add more drops of water gradually, taking care not to make the mixture thin. Beat till the mixture turns a little whitish and fluffy.
3. Put half the beaten coffee in each cup.
4. Strain milk in a pan or degchi. Add water. Keep on fire to boil.
5. When the milk-water mixture boils, reduce flame & simmer for a minute.
6. Remove from fire and pour into cups from a little height to get a frothy coffee. Stir. Sprinkle some drinking chocolate. Serve immediately.

VEGETARIAN SANDWICHES

from

Nita Mehta

Open Pasta Sandwich

An interesting snack!

<u>Serves 4</u>

1½ cups boiled noodles or spaghetti
1 tbsp butter
1 onion - finely chopped
3-4 flakes garlic - crushed & chopped
1 green chilli - deseeded & finely cut
1/3 cup tomato ketchup (add according to taste)
50 gm (8 tbsp) cheese - grated
4 slices bread - toasted crisp & buttered
salt, pepper, chilli powder to taste

Cottage Cheese Sandwiches : page 25

1. Heat butter in a small kadhai. Fry onions till transparent.
2. Add garlic paste. Saute for a few seconds.
3. Add spaghetti or noodles and mix well.
4. Add grated cheese, leaving some for the topping.
5. Add green chilli, ketchup, salt, pepper and red chilli powder. Remove from fire.
6. Butter the freshly toasted slices of bread. Spread the spaghetti mixture on the toasted bread.
7. Grate some cheese finely over it.
8. Cut into halves and serve as open toasts.

Swiss Circles : page 44

Spicy Beans with Cottage Cheese

A light snack!

<u>Serves 6</u>

6 slices of bread - toasted crisp & buttered
1¼ cups (1 small tin) baked beans
1 small onion - finely chopped
1 green chilli - deseeded & finely chopped
A few sprigs of coriander leaves - chopped
a few drops capsico sauce - optional
6 thin slices of paneer (cottage cheese)
3 cabbage leaves - torn roughly into two pieces
some chaat masala

1. Mash baked beans **roughly** with a fork.
2. Mix in onion, green chilli, coriander and capsico sauce. Add ¼ tsp salt or to taste.
3. In 1 tbsp butter, shallow fry the paneer slices lightly in a non-stick pan on both sides. Shift the paneer slices and add the cabbage leaves. Saute for a few seconds.
4. Remove paneer from pan, sprinkle chaat masala on both the sides of the paneer.
5. Spread butter on slices of toast.
6. Arrange a piece of cabbage leaf on each toast.
7. Arrange a slice of cottage cheese on it.
8. Spread some bean mixture over the paneer slice.
9. Cut each toast diagonally into two triangles. Serve.

Grilled Cheese & Vegetable Sandwich

Picture on page 71

Serves 2

4 slices bread, 2 cubes cheese (50 gm) - grated
butter - enough to spread
1 tbsp mayonnaise - optional
3-4 tbsp grated cabbage, 3-4 tbsp grated carrot

1. Spread softened butter properly on both sides of a slice or if you like, spread mayonnaise on one side and butter on the other side of a slice.
2. Spread some cabbage on the mayonnaise. Sprinkle some grated carrot.
3. Grate a cube of cheese over the carrots. Cover with another slice, keeping the buttered side outside. Press gently.
4. Empty the oven, keeping only the wire rack. Preheat oven to **maximum**, with **both** the heating coils 'ON'. Place sandwich on the wire rack and grill till golden brown. Turn the sandwich carefully if required.

Note : In the absence of an oven, heat some butter in a non stick pan. Place the sandwich. Cover the pan & keep on medium flame till golden.

Toasted Club Sandwiches

Picture on cover

Serves 2

6 bread slices - toasted in a toaster or put under a grill till brown
2 tbsp mayonnaise, 1 tbsp thick cream
4 tbsp shredded carrot, 4 tbsp shredded cabbage
2 lettuce leaves, 2 cheese slices
1 firm tomato - cut into slices, a few kheera (cucumber) slices
salt & pepper to taste, olives, cherries or grapes for garnishing

1. Mix mayonnaise, cream and shredded carrots and cabbage. Add a little salt and pepper to taste. Spread half of this mixture on a toast.
2. Put a lettuce on it. Put some tomato slices on it. Sprinkle salt and pepper.
3. Put another toast on the tomatoes. Put a slice of cheese on the second toast. Cover cheese with a lettuce leaf. Arrange kheera slices on it and sprinkle salt and pepper on it.
4. Put the last toast. Press well and cut into 4 triangles. Secure each triangle with a tooth pick. Serve them upright. Repeat with other toasts.

Mushroom Triangles

An evening snack!

Serves 3

100 gms mushrooms - washed & sliced finely
3/4 cup water
1 tbsp butter
1 small onion - chopped
1 tbsp flour (maida)
salt and pepper to taste
3 slices bread - toasted and buttered

1. Boil mushrooms in ½ cup water for a few minutes, till slightly tender.
2. Fry onion in butter till transparent.
3. Add flour and stir for a minute. Reduce flame.
4. Add mushrooms along with the water, stirring continuously. Mix well.
5. Add salt and pepper. Cook till thick. Remove from fire.
6. Spread on buttered toasted bread. Cut diagonally into 4 triangles and serve as open sandwiches, garnished with a fresh coriander or mint leaf.

Cottage Cheese Sandwich

Picture on page 17
A low calorie, all time favourite sandwich!

Serves 2

75 gm paneer (cottage cheese) - grated
2 tbsp (or even more) coriander - finely chopped
1 tsp ginger-garlic paste
2 tsp tomato ketchup
salt & pepper to taste
4 slices of bread

1. Lightly mix grated paneer with lots of green coriander, a little ginger garlic paste and tomato ketchup. Add salt & pepper to taste.
2. Spread paneer mix on a plain or a lightly buttered slice.
3. Spread tomato ketchup on another slice & place on the paneer slice.
4. Press. Cut into 3 triangular pieces. (See pages 10-11). Repeat with the other slices. Arrange upright so that the filling shows, on a bed of shredded cabbage & carrot.

Apple & Cheese Sandwiches

Delicious, Iron rich sandwiches!

Serves 4

8 slices of brown bread
2 apples - peeled, cored and grated
1 tsp lemon juice
50 gm cheese - grated
4 tbsp (100 gm) cheese spread
½ tsp capsico sauce
½ tsp salt, ¼ tsp pepper or to taste

1. Sprinkle lemon juice over the grated apple. Mix lightly with a fork.
2. Add grated cheese, cheese spread, capsico sauce, salt & pepper.
3. Divide the mixture into four and spread evenly over 4 slices.
4. Cover with the other 4 slices. Press well. Divide into two.

Note : Ordinary bread may be used if brown bread is not available.

Macaroni Open Sandwich

Picture on page 36

<u>Serves 4</u>

4 slices bread - toasted & buttered
1 cup boiled macaroni
2 tsp tomato ketchup
salt, pepper to taste
3/4 cup fresh tomato puree (grind 2 big tomatoes)
2 flakes garlic - chopped and crushed
1 cube (¼ cup) grated cheese
a few spring onion leaves cut into fine rings - to garnish

1. Boil ½ cup macaroni to get 1 cup boiled macaroni. Drain.
2. Thicken the tomato puree & garlic in a small kadhai. Remove from fire.
3. Add tomato sauce, salt and pepper. Mix. Add macaroni, mix gently.
4. Spread the macaroni mixture on a buttered toast. Sprinkle **finely** grated cheese. Garnish with spring onions. Cut into two pieces and serve.

Sandwich Faces

Interesting for a child's B'day party!
Picture on page 53

Serves 12

6 slices of brown bread, 6 slices of white bread - cut into circles with a biscuit
cutter or a sharp edged lid of a bottle
butter - enough to spread

FILLINGS
2 tbsp any jam
2 tbsp poodina chutney
2 tbsp cheese spread

FACES
1 carrot - finely grated (for hair)
¼ capsicum - cut into tiny squares (for eyes)
6 glace cherries - cut into half (for nose)
a firm tomato - cut into small thickish strips (for mouth)

GARNISHING
a few lettuce or cabbage leaves - cut into fine strips (shredded)
3 small red radish or small firm tomatoes - cut into flowers

1. Cut two circles from each slice of white and brown bread. Butter all circles. Spread jam on two brown circles and cover each brown circle with a white circle. Similarly make round sandwiches of white and brown bread with chutney and cheese spread. Keep aside.

2. Sprinkle the finely cut lettuce or cabbage on a platter. Place the sandwiches with the white side up, on the bed of cabbage or lettuce, leaving at least an inch between one another.

3. To make faces, arrange a few shreds of **finely** grated carrot on the top $\frac{1}{4}$ th portion of the sandwich rounds to make the hair.

4. Place $\frac{1}{2}$ of a glace cherry to make the nose.

5. Arrange tiny squares of green capsicum for the eyes. Cut a small, semi circled, thickish strip for the mouth.

6. Cut deep (VVV) v's from the centre of a small tomato or red radish and gently pull apart to make roses. Place small radish roses in between the faces, on the lettuce or cabbage bed.

CORN & MUSHROOM TOASTS

An evening snack!

Serves 8

½ cup (100 gms) of canned sweet corn
100 gms of mushrooms - washed & cut into thin slices
4 slices of toasted bread - buttered & cut into four pieces
1/3 tsp salt, ¼ tsp pepper or to taste, a dash of capsico sauce
2 tbsp of thick cream or lightly whipped fresh malai
a few coriander leaves - to garnish

1. Heat 1 tbsp butter in a small kadhai. Fry the sliced mushrooms, till light brown. Add tinned corn, salt & pepper. Stir for a minute.
2. Remove from heat and stir in cream & capsico sauce.
3. Spread a little butter on the toasted bread and cut into 4 pieces. Spread some corn filling over the toasts. Garnish with a coriander leaf. Serve.

Note : Transfer the left over sweet corn in a stainless steel box and store it in the freezer compartment of your refrigerator for a month or so.

Brown Vegetable Sandwiches

Picture on backcover
Quick and simple to prepare!

Serves 2

4 tbsp finely shredded cabbage
4 tbsp grated carrot
2 tbsp ready made mayonnaise or butter
1 cube (25 gm) cheese
4 brown bread slices - crust removed

1. Spread mayonnaise or softened butter on 4 slices of brown bread.
2. Sprinkle some cabbage on a slice spread with mayonnaise. Now sprinkle a layer of grated carrots on the cabbage.
3. Grate some cheese over it.
4. Cover with another slice spread generously with mayonnaise or butter.
5. Press well. Cut into three diagonally, as shown on pages 10-11.
6. Arrange on a bed of lettuce strips in a serving plate.

Vegetable Burgers with Cole Slaw

Picture on page 35
The perfect burger!

Serves 6

6 fresh burger buns
a few lettuce or cabbage leaves - hard stem removed & torn roughly into two
1 small cucumber - cut into slices without peeling
¼ cup white vinegar mixed with ¼ tsp sugar & ¼ tsp salt
a few onion & tomato slices (very thin slices)

COLE SLAW

2-3 tbsp ready made mayonnaise, 1 tbsp fresh cream or malai (beaten well)
1 cup very finely shredded cabbage, ½ carrot - grated
2-3 drops lemon juice, salt and pepper to taste

BURGER (TIKKI)

4 big potatoes - boiled & grated, 1 onion - finely chopped, 1 tbsp butter
2 small carrots - chopped, 10-12 french beans - cut into small cubes
3 bread slices - sides removed and crumbled, 3 tsp ready made mustard paste
1 tsp salt or to taste, ½ tsp amchoor, ½ tsp garam masala, ½ tsp red chilli pd.

1. Soak unpeeled cucumber slices in the vinegar mix and keep aside.
2. Prepare cole slaw by mixing mayonnaise & fresh cream in a large bowl. Mix finely shredded cabbage & carrot. Add lemon juice, salt & pepper.
3. Pressure cook carrots & beans in 1/3 cup water to give one whistle. Keep on fire for 2-3 minutes. Remove from fire. After the pressure drops, mash the hot vegetables. If there is any water left in the cooker, mash on fire so that the water dries. Heat 1 tbsp butter in a kadhai. Add chopped onion and fry till transparent. Add carrots & beans. Add spices. Cook for 2-3 min. Mix boiled and grated potatoes. Remove from fire.
4. Add crumbled bread. Check seasonings. Make balls & shape into tikkis (burgers). Shallow fry in 2-3 tbsp oil in a non stick pan, till brown & crisp.
5. To assemble, cut the buns into half, saute in a little oil or butter in the pan. Keep pressing the buns till soft. Remove from pan.
6. Spread a little mustard paste on the lower portion of the bun, if you like the flavour of mustard. Arrange a lettuce leaf. Place a hot tikki on it & then spread some cole slaw. Arrange a slice of pickled cucumber, onion & tomato. Sprinkle salt & pepper. Cover with the other piece of bun, tilting it slightly such that the filling shows. Fix a tooth pick if desired.

CREAM-CURD SURPRISE

Serves 3

6 slices bread - toasted & buttered
½ cup thick curd of full cream milk - hung for 10 min. in a muslin cloth
2 tbsp fresh cream or fresh malai (well beaten)
1 small tomato - pulp removed & very finely chopped
½ small capsicum - very finely chopped
2 tbsp grated carrot
2 tbsp finely chopped cucumber
½ tsp salt, ¼ tsp pepper, ½ tsp mustard powder or to taste

1. Hang curd. Squeeze lightly. Mix curd & cream. Beat well.
2. Add finely chopped tomato, capsicum, carrot & cucumber. Add salt, pepper and mustard powder to taste.
3. Toast the slices & butter lightly. Spread filling evenly on 3 slices of toast.
4. Cover with the remaining toasts. Press together firmly. Cut & serve.

Vegetable Burgers with Cole Slaw : page 32

Sandwiched Peas

<u>Serves 4</u>

8 slices bread - lightly buttered
1 cup peas - shelled, ½ cup grated paneer (50 gm)
1 onion - chopped finely, 1 green chilli - deseeded & chopped finely
¼ tsp roasted jeera powder, ¼ tsp chilli powder, ½ tsp salt or to taste

1. Heat 1 tbsp oil. Add onions & green chillies. Cook till transparent.
2. Add peas, jeera powder, chilli & salt. Cover & cook till done. Add a few tbsp water if required while cooking. Remove from fire. Mash roughly.
3. Add grated paneer & and mix well. Check seasonings, keeping it a little on the higher side, since it is between bread slices.
4. Spread a layer of pea mix on the unbuttered side of four slices.
5. Cover with the remaining slices with the buttered side outside. Press firmly. Grill, by placing on the wire rack of a hot oven or toast in a sandwich toaster. Serve hot.

Macaroni Open Sandwich : page 27

Rainbow Sandwiches

Serves 2-3

3 slices of white bread - buttered lightly
2 tbsp tomato sauce
2 tbsp poodina (mint) chutney - page 92
½ cup besan (gram flour)
½ tsp salt, a pinch of baking pd., 1 tsp lemon juice
oil for frying

1. Make a semi thick batter of besan, salt, baking powder, lemon juice with 1/3 cup water approximately. Beat well.
2. Spread chutney on one slice on the buttered side.
3. Cover with another slice and spread tomato sauce.
4. Cover with the last slice. Press well.
5. Dip the sandwich into the besan batter. See that the batter covers all sides and deep fry. Cut into four long pieces and serve hot.

CHEESE-RAISIN SANDWICH

Children love these sandwiches and so do the adults!

Serves 4

8 slices white or brown bread - lightly buttered
4 tbsp raisins (kishmish) - soaked in water
3 cubes (75 gm) cheese - grated
3 tbsp milk
3 tbsp mayonnaise

1.   Soak the raisins in warm water for 5-7 minutes. Drain off.
2.   Blend the grated cheese with milk and mayonnaise.
3.   Add soaked and properly drained raisins.
4.   Butter all the slices lightly. Spread some filling on a slice and cover with another slice.
5.   Cut into two and serve.

Note : You may reduce the amount of raisins (kishmish) for adults.

Jumbo Sandwich

Picture on page 72
An ideal breakfast for the family!

Serves 6

1 French loaf or cheese loaf (any boat shaped loaf) - cut into two horizontally
2-3 tbsp butter - softened
(200 gm) 1 small tin baked beans - 1¼ cup
2 tbsp oil
2 onions - chopped finely
1 capsicum - chopped finely
salt, pepper - to taste
½ tsp chilli sauce
2 tbsp coriander leaves - cut finely
2 cubes cheese - grated

1. Slightly scoop out both the bread pieces, leaving a border of 1" all around to from a boat. (The scooped out bread is not needed in this recipe, but add it to any tikkis, koftas or any snack to make it crisp.)
2. Soften butter and apply to the scooped out surface and the border of both the boats.
3. Heat oil in a pan and add onions and fry till pink.
4. Add capsicums, stir for a minute.
5. Add salt, pepper and chilli sauce. **Remove from fire.**
6. Add baked beans. Mix well.
7. Pile this filling into the scooped out hollows of the French loaf.
8. Sprinkle grated cheese and some coriander leaves on the top.
9. Grill for 3-4 minutes or microwave at medium power for 2 minutes till the cheese melts slightly. Serve hot.

Corn Footlong

Picture on cover

Serves 10-12

1 French loaf - cut into half horizontally
2 tsp mustard paste

FLAVOURED BUTTER (MIX TOGETHER)
4 tbsp softened butter, 1 tsp saboot kali mirch (black peppercorns) - crushed
2-3 flakes garlic - chopped & crushed, 2 tbsp finely chopped coriander

TOPPING
1 tbsp butter, 2 tbsp cheese spread
1 cup tinned or cooked corn (kernel)
1 capsicum - finely chopped
1 large onion - finely chopped
salt, pepper to taste
4-6 tbsp mozzarella cheese - grated
1 tsp oregano or red chilli flakes

1. Mix all ingredients given under flavoured butter and beat well to soften the butter.
2. Cut the French loaf horizontally to get 2 long pieces.
3. Butter one piece with half of the flavoured butter. Spread some mustard paste on the buttered footlong and keep aside.
4. Preheat the oven to 180°C.
5. To prepare the topping heat 1 tbsp butter in a pan or kadhai. Add onion. Fry till soft. Add corn, salt & pepper. Stir well to mix. Remove from fire.
6. Add capsicum and cheese spread to the hot mixture.
7. Spread corn filling on the buttered foot long.
8. Grate mozzarella cheese over it and sprinkle some oregano.
9. At serving time, grill at 180°C for 10-12 minutes or till cheese melts and the bread turns crisp.
10. To serve, cut into 1½" thick slices.
11. Repeat with the other piece of the loaf.

Swiss Circles

Picture on page 18

<u>Serves 4-6</u>

5 slices of soft fresh bread
100 gms paneer - grated
1 capsicum - finely chopped
1 tbsp butter
2 green chillies - deseeded & finely chopped
1 tbsp tomato ketchup
a pinch garam masala
½ tsp salt, ¼ tsp chilli powder

SEALING PASTE
2 tsp cornflour or maida mixed with 2 tbsp water to make a paste

1. Grate paneer and add all other ingredients to make a paste.
2. Cut the sides of a slice, keep it flat on a rolling board.
3. Press, applying pressure with a rolling pin so that the holes of the bread close.
4. Apply a layer of the filling and roll the slice carefully.
5. Seal the edges with cornflour paste.
6. Keep the roll, rolled up in a thin cloth or a piece of cling film for at least 10-15 minutes.
7. Deep fry one roll at a time, in hot oil till golden. Cut into 4 pieces and serve hot.

Note : If you do not want fried circles, apply softened butter on the roll and cut into 3 pieces. Bake on a greased wire race or in an oven proof glass dish for 15 minutes till light brown.

Yoghurt Toasts

Delightful Breakfast!

Serves 4

8 slices bread - buttered very lightly
2 cups thick fresh curds (prepared from full cream milk) - hung for 1 hour
1 onion - finely chopped
1 tomato - pulp removed & finely chopped
1 capsicum - finely chopped
½ tsp bhuna jeera - powdered
½ tsp salt and pepper or to taste

1. Hang the curds in a muslin cloth for 1 hour.
2. Mix curd, onion, tomato, capsicum salt, pepper & powdered jeera.
3. Spread 2 tbsp of the mixture on the unbuttered side of a slice. Cover with another slice, keeping the buttered side on the outside.
4. Toast on a non-stick pan on both the sides. Remove when sides are lightly browned. Cut into two and serve.

TEEN BURGERS

Serves 4

2 tbsp oil
2 onions - chopped finely, 1 capsicum - chopped finely
(200 gm) 1 small can baked beans - 1¼ cup
2-3 sprigs of finely chopped coriander leaves
½ tsp pepper powder and salt, ½ tsp chilli sauce
4 soft burger buns
2 tbsp butter, 2 cubes (50 gm) cheese - grated

1. Divide buns into two halves. Scoop out, leaving ½" border all around.
2. Heat oil in a kadhai and fry the onions until softened.
3. Add capsicum. Stir for 1 minute. Remove from fire. Add baked beans.
4. Add salt, pepper and chilli sauce.
5. Toast the scooped sides on a non-stick pan with some butter.
6. Pile some bean mixture in the scooped out hollows. Grate some cheese over it. Grill or microwave on medium power for 1 minute.

Moong Toast

Breakfast with an Indian touch!

Serves 2

1 cup dhuli Moong dal - soaked for 1-2 hours only and ground to a paste
2-4 green chillies
a bunch of coriander leaves - chopped finely
½ tsp baking powder
1 tbsp besan
1½ tsp lemon juice
4-5 tbsp oil
4 slices bread - lightly buttered
1¼ tsp salt or to taste

1. Drain and grind dal along with chillies to a fine batter.
2. Mix moong dal paste, coriander leaves, baking powder, besan, lemon juice and salt.
3. Heat 4-5 tbsp oil in a non stick pan.
4. Butter the slices lightly.
5. Spread the dal mixture on the slice on the buttered side.
6. Invert the slice with the dal side down in the pan. Spread some dal paste on the upper side too with a spoon. Shallow fry on both sides until light brown.
7. Remove from pan and into any shape as given on pages 10 or 11.
8. Serve hot with tomato sauce or mint chutney given on page 92.

East-West Sandwich

<u>Serves 4</u>

6 slices - lightly buttered

POTATO-PEA FILLING

1 potato - boiled, peeled & grated, ¼ cup peas - boiled and mashed
2 tbsp green mint (poodina) chutney, salt & pepper to taste

CHEESE FILLING

1 onion - chopped finely, 1 small capsicum - chopped finely
2 cubes cheese - grated, 3 tbsp mayonnaise

1. Mix together peas, potatoes, chutney, salt and pepper. Keep aside.
2. Mix grated cheese, onions, capsicum & mayonnaise together.
3. Apply the pea-potato filling on one slice of bread and cover with the second slice. Press together.
4. Spread cheese filling on the second slice and cover with the third. Press. Similarly make another sandwich with the other three slices.
5. Remove sides, cut into three pieces and serve upright in a serving platter.

Party Sandwich

Ideal for a tea-party!
Picture on page 54

Picture on page 54

Serves 10

COVERING
1½ cups thick curd *prepared from full cream milk*
salt, pepper to taste, 1 tsp powdered sugar

YELLOW CHEESE FILLING
50 gms paneer
2 tbsp finely grated cucumber or carrot
salt, pepper to taste
1 tbsp milk, few drops of yellow colour or a pinch haldi

RED TOMATO FILLING
2 tomatoes - pureed in a grinder
2 tbsp tomato sauce
¼ tsp salt, ¼ tsp pepper

GREEN MINT CHUTNEY
(½ cup) ½ bunch poodina (mint) leaves
1 cup hara dhania (coriander) leaves
1 green chilli, 1 onion - sliced
1 tsp sugar, salt and amchoor to taste

OTHER INGREDIENTS
12 slices of fresh bread (sides removed)
butter - enough to spread
fresh coriander leaves & a few black grapes for garnishing

1. Hang curd **(prepared from full cream milk)** for ½ hour in a thin cloth. Beat well along with salt, sugar & pepper till smooth. Keep in the fridge.
2. To prepare yellow filling, grate paneer. Mix everything to make a paste of spreading consistency. Add some yellow colour. Keep filling aside.
3. Grind tomatoes to a puree in a mixer. Cook puree in a small pan till thick. Add tomato sauce, salt & pepper. Cook for 1 min. Keep red filling aside.
4. Grind all ingredients of the mint chutney to a fine paste with some water.

Sandwich Faces : page 28

5. In a longish serving plate, arrange 3 slices bread joining each other.
6. Spread cheese filling on each slice. Butter 3 more slices and cover the cheese filling with the buttered side of the slices.
7. Spread green chutney generously. Cover with 3 buttered slices.
8. Spread red filling generously. Cover with 3 more buttered slices of bread.
9. Cover this loaf with beaten curd.
10. Draw a clean fork lengthwise on the curd, across the sandwich in the centre. Draw lines on the sides also with a fork.
11. Dip small coriander leaves in cold water for 10 minutes. Arrange 2 rows of open coriander leaves on both sides.
12. In the centre, place cherry or grape halves on the fork lines, if you like.
13. Cut a tomato slice into four pieces, arrange one on each corner.
14. Refrigerate for atleast 1-2 hours or even more, before serving. To serve, cut into slices.

Party Sandwich : page 51

Curd Vegetable Fingers

<u>Serves 4</u>

1 cup of thick curd (hung in a cloth for 1-2 hours)
2 tbsp malai or cream
4 tbsp grated cabbage
4 tbsp grated carrot
1 small capsicum - very finely chopped
2 tbsp onion - finely chopped
¼ tsp mustard powder or prepared mustard
½ tsp worcestershire sauce - optional
2 tsp tomato sauce
4 slices of bread - lightly toasted
salt & pepper to taste

1. Tie curd in a muslin cloth and keep it tied for 1-2 hours till the water gets drained properly.
2. Beat together drained curd & cream till smooth.
3. Add all seasonings, grated and chopped vegetables.
4. Spread the mix on the lightly toasted slices.
6. To grill, place on the wire rack of a hot oven, grill for 2-3 minutes.
5. Remove crust from bread slices and cut into finger shaped pieces. Serve hot.

Grilled Chilli Cheese Sandwiches

Pickled chillies should be made a day in advance, but can be stored for a week.

Serves 2

4 slices bread
cheese spread - enough to spread on 4 slices
2 cheese slices or 50 gm cheese - grated
softened butter - enough to spread on 4 slices

PICKLED CUCUMBER & GREEN CHILLIES (shake well together in a bottle)
¼ cup white vinegar , ½ tsp salt, ½ tsp sugar
½ kheera - cut into slices without peeling, 1 thick green chilli - round slices

1. Spread butter on one side & cheese spread on the other side of all slices.
2. Arrange 4 pickled kheera slices, prepared a day earlier on the cheese spread on 2 bread slices. Sprinkle a few pickled green chilli rings. Spread grated cheese. Cover with another slice, properly buttered on outer side.
3. Press. Place the prepared sandwich on the **wire rack of a hot oven & grill** till golden on both sides. Serve with cole slaw as given on page 32.

NON VEGETARIAN
SANDWICHES
from
Meenakshi Ahuja

Ham-Tomato Sandwich

<u>Serves 4</u>

4 slices bread
2 tbsp butter
2 thick slices ham
1 tomato - cut into round slices
few drops worcestershire sauce
1 onion - cut into round slices
pinch of pepper and salt

1. Spread one side of the bread slices with some butter.
2. Sandwich together with the slice of ham in between. Keep aside.
3. Add 1 tbsp butter to the frying pan and keep on fire.
4. Add tomato, onion slices and the sandwich.
5. Cook for 2 minutes on either side until crisp.
6. Arrange tomato and onion slices on top of the sandwich, sprinkle worcestershire sauce, pepper and salt.

Chicken Burgers

Serves 4

4 soft burger buns
1 medium sized onion - finely chopped
300 gm chicken meat - minced
3 heaped tbsp white bread crumbs or crumbled bread
1 tbsp cornflour, 1 egg
1 tbsp ready made mustard paste, 1 onion - sliced

1. Melt 1 tbsp butter in a frying pan and fry the chopped onions until pink.
2. Remove from fire. Mix chicken meat, bread crumbs and seasonings.
3. Add egg and cornflour to bind the mixture.
4. On a floured board, form the mixture into 4 round burgers.
5. Heat some oil in a frying pan and fry the burger on each side.
6. Split the buns, toss in some butter in a pan till soft. Remove from pan & spread some mustard paste on the lower piece.
7. Place a burger and a slice of onion in each. If you have a microwave, micro on medium power for 1 minute. Serve burger with a green salad.

Cheese & Luncheon Meat Fingers

Serves 6

4 slices white bread - toasted & buttered
2 slices brown bread
2 slices of meat
2-4 slices of cheese
25 gm butter
a little mustard paste

1. Toast the slices of bread and spread with butter.
2. Arrange meat on two slices of white bread.
3. Spread a little mustard paste. Cover with brown bread.
4. Place 1-2 slices of cheese. Top with the remaining slices of white bread.
5. Cut into fingers and serve with tomato sauce.

Mock Pizza

Serves 4

4 slices of bread - remove sides
1 capsicum - sliced
4 tbsp tomato sauce, a piece of crushed garlic, ¼ tsp crushed ajwain
2 cubes of cheese - grated
4 slices of salami
4 mushrooms
25 gm butter

1. Mix tomato sauce with crushed garlic and ajwain.
2. Spread the slices with butter.
3. Spread 1 tbsp tomato sauce on each slice.
4. Place on a greased baking tray. Place a slice of salami, a slice of capsicum, then a whole mushroom dotted with butter.
5. Sprinkle cheese & bake in a preheated oven at 190°C for 10-15 min.

Yoghurt Prawn Sandwich

Serves 2

2 slices of firm white or brown bread
2 tbsp of hung yoghurt (tie 1 cup yoghurt in a muslin cloth for 15 minutes)
50 gms prawns - devein & saute in butter with salt and pepper
1 tsp finely chopped capsicum and onion
¼ tsp salt, pepper
few lettuce leaves - if not available, substitute with cabbage

1. Saute prawns in 1 tsp butter with a little salt and pepper.
2. Beat yoghurt. Blend salt, pepper, capsicum and onion into the yoghurt.
3. Mix prawns with the yoghurt, keeping aside a few for garnishing.
4. Spread the bread slices with some butter.
5. Arrange lettuce leaves on the buttered bread.
6. Place yoghurt-prawns mixture on the lettuce, then garnish with the remaining prawns. Cut into squares if desired.

Sandwich Loaf

<u>Serves 8</u>

1 loaf bread - (a day old)
1 cup cooked chicken - chopped finely
1 cup cooked ham - chopped finely
2 cups mayonnaise - page 94
½ tsp salt or to taste
½ tsp pepper
½ tsp mustard powder
1 cup grated cheese

1. Trim crusts from loaf of bread.
2. Slice off the top and scoop out the loaf, leaving 1 inch shell all around.
3. Mix the cooked chicken, ham, mayonnaise, cheese, salt, pepper and mustard. Fill the mixture into the loaf of bread.
4. Replace the top slice and chill for ½ hour.
5. Serve on a platter and slice like a loaf of bread.

Devilled Ham Sandwich

Serves 2

2 thick slices of brown bread
4 slices of cooked ham
2 tbsp mayonnaise
1 cucumber - cut into thin slices
2 cheese cubes - cut into slices

1. Spread butter on the bread slice.
2. Spread ham slices with mayonnaise and roll up.
3. Place cucumber slices slightly overlapping along the edges of bread slice.
4. Place the ham rolls in the centre - 2 rolls on each slice.
5. Top with wedge shaped slices of cheese.

Salami Sandwich

Serves 2

2 slices of brown or white bread - buttered
2 lettuce or cabbage leaves
4 slices of salami
a few onion slices - separated into rings
2 tbsp shredded cabbage mixed with 2 tbsp of mayonnaise
1 tomato cut into wedges - deseeded

1. Spread butter on the slices.
2. Cover with a lettuce leaf.
3. Arrange salami slices. Arrange some cabbage-mayonnaise mix on the salami.
4. Garnish with onion rings and wedges of tomato.

BACON BURGERS

Serves 8

½ kg minced meat
3 tbsp fresh bread crumbs
1 egg beaten
salt, pepper, chilli powder, garam masala - to taste
1 small bunch coriander leaves - cut finely
1-2 green chillies - cut finely
8 rashers of bacon
tooth picks
oil for frying
8 round soft buns
butter - to spread
tomato ketchup
1 tsp mustard paste

1. Mix together the minced meat, bread crumbs, egg, green chillies, coriander and seasonings.
2. On a floured board, form the mixture into 8 round cutlets.
3. Wrap a rasher of bacon round each cutlet and secure with tooth picks, inserted on the sides.
4. Heat oil in a frying pan and fry the burgers for about 4 minutes on each side. Remove the tooth picks.
5. Slit the buns and butter them.
6. Put the burgers between the buttered rolls, top with a tsp of tomato ketchup and mustard paste.

Double Decker

<u>Serves 4</u>

12 slices of bread - lightly toasted & buttered
2 cheese cubes - grated
2 eggs - boiled and sliced

CHICKEN-PEA FILLING
1 cup chicken pieces - boiled and shredded
½ cup peas - boiled and mashed
juice of 1 lemon, salt & pepper

MAYONNAISE FILLING
½ carrot - scraped and grated, ½ cup cabbage - shredded
½ capsicums - thinly sliced
½ cup moong - sprouted & boiled
4 tbsp mayonnaise

Grilled Cheese & Vegetable Sandwiches : page 22

1. Mix peas, chicken, salt, pepper and lime juice.
2. Mix the grated carrot, cabbage, capsicums, moong sprouts and mayonnaise.
3. Spread the chicken mixture on one slice.
4. Place a second slice and spread the mayonnaise mixture.
5. Place a few egg slices and top with grated cheese.
6. Cover with the third slice of bread.
7. Cut into a triangle and serve.
8. Repeat with the remaining nine slices.

Jumbo Sandwich : page 40

Devils Delight

<u>Serves 9</u>

9 slices sandwich bread - toasted and trimmed
½ cup thousand island dressing - page 92
1 small can pineapple - drained & crushed
9 slices of salami
9 slices of ham
3 cheese cubes or 9 slices of cheese
a small papaya or melon - scoop out balls
a few lettuce leaves

1. Place the toasted slices on a tray and place a lettuce leaf.
2. Spread with thousand island dressing.
3. Spread crushed pineapple.
4. Place a slice of ham, then salami and cheese cut into triangles on it.
5. Serve garnished with fresh fruit balls of melon or papaya.

Chicken Hawaii

Serves 2

2 round buns
2 pineapple rings
1 cup boiled shredded chicken
½ cup shredded cabbage
½ cup mayonnaise
2 radish roses
2 carrot curls

1. Cut buns in half and toast both halves on bottom half.
2. Put a slice of pineapple.
3. Mix chicken, cabbage and mayonnaise.
4. Top pineapple slice with the chicken mixture.
5. Lean the other half of the bun on one side.
6. Garnish with radish roses and carrot curls.

Tuna Sandwiches

Serves 12

1 tin tuna
1 tbsp finely chopped onion
¼ cup finely chopped parsley, celery or coriander leaves
2 boiled eggs - chopped finely
1 tsp mustard paste
1 tbsp mayonnaise
12 slices of bread - brown or white

1. Drain the tuna and mix in a bowl with onion and parsley.
2. Mix in the mustard paste, chopped eggs along with the mayonnaise into the tuna mixture.
3. Spread the mixture on six slices and sandwich with the remaining slices.
4. Cut into desired shapes and serve on a platter.

Sandwiches with Chicken left over

Serves 6

1 cup chicken pieces
½ cup thick white sauce - page 93
1 egg
1 onion - chopped finely
6 slices bread - toasted or plain
25 gms butter
salt to taste
pepper to taste

1. In a pan add butter and fry the onions till pink.
2. Add eggs and mix well. Add salt and pepper. Remove from fire.
3. Mix the chicken pieces and white sauce.
4. Spread on slices of bread or toast.

Shrimp Sandwiches

<u>Serves 5</u>

5 slices buttered bread
½ cup chopped cooked shrimp
1 can tuna-flaked
¼ cup finely chopped celery or coriander
1 tsp lemon juice
2/3 cup mayonnaise
10 whole cooked shrimps
a few capsicum strips

1. Combine chopped shrimp, flaked tuna, celery, lemon juice and mayonnaise.
2. Spread filling on each bread slice.
3. Garnish each sandwich with 2 whole shrimps and 2 capsicum strips.

Pyramid Sandwiches

Serves 4

4 slices bread- sides removed & buttered
½ cup boiled & shredded chicken
¼ cup capsicum - cut into tiny pieces
2 slices ham
2 slices cheese
½ cup thick cream or hung curd
salt, pepper

1. Mix boiled chicken and capsicum. Sprinkle with salt and pepper.
2. Place two slices on a tray. Spread the chicken-capsicum filling.
3. Place a ham and cheese slice and cover with another slice. Cut sandwiches into half diagonally.
4. Place 2 triangles short sides, back to back on a plate.
5. Whip cream till thick, put in an icing bag and garnish sandwiches.

Egg Cheese Toast

<u>Serves 4</u>

4 slices of bread
1 egg
2 tbsp cornflour
4 tbsp grated cheese
¼ tsp mustard powder, ¼ tsp chilli powder
pinch of soda bi-carb
½ tsp salt, pepper or to taste
oil for deep frying

1. Beat the egg lightly.
2. Mix cornflour, cheese, mustard powder, chilli powder, soda bi-carb and salt & pepper. It should be a thick paste.
3. Apply this paste over the bread slices. Deep fry in oil. The toast will puff up. Cut into halves.
4. Serve with tomato ketchup.

Junglee Sandwiches

Serves 6

6 slices bread - lightly buttered
2 flakes garlic
1 cup boiled shredded chicken
3 tbsp thousand island dressing - page 92
3 green chillies - chopped
1 sprig coriander leaves - chopped
¼ tsp salt
3 cheese slices

1. Rub the garlic in a mixing bowl to give a mild garlic flavour to the filling.
2. Add chicken, thousand island, green chillies, coriander and salt.
3. Apply the mixture on three slices of bread.
4. Place cheese slices on the top and cover with the remaining slices. Press together.
5. Cut into any desired shape and serve.

Baked Ham & Tomato Sandwiches

Serves 4

1 French loaf or 4 hot dog buns
8 slices smoked ham
2 large tomatoes - sliced
4 tbsp mayonnaise
½ tsp worcestershire sauce
1 tbsp mustard
½ tsp soya sauce
3 spring onions - finely chopped
100 gms cheese - grated
1 tsp salt
½ tsp pepper

1. Heat the oven to 200°C/400°F.
2. In a bowl mix together the mayonnaise, mustard, worcestershire, soya sauce, spring onion, cheese, salt and pepper to taste.
3. Cut the French loaf in half across, then cut each half into 2 pieces. Cut off the round ends, so that you have 4 rectangular pieces of bread.
4. Spread the cheese mixture over the cut surfaces of the bread.
5. Lay 2 ham slices on each piece of bread, then top with tomato slices and season with salt and pepper.
6. Wrap each open sandwich in a piece of foil and arrange these side by side on a baking tray.
7. Bake for 30 minutes or until the cheese mixture is melted and bubbling. Serve hot garnished with the reserved spring onions.

TOMATO EGG TOASTS

<u>Serves 4</u>

4 slices of buttered toast
4 tomatoes - sliced, 1 hard boiled egg - cut into slices

CHEESE SAUCE
1 tbsp butter, 1 tbsp flour
1 cup milk
¼ tsp each of salt, pepper & mustard powder
1 cube cheese - grated

1. Melt the butter in a pan. Add flour and stir for a minute.
2. Gradually add the milk, stirring and bring to a boil. Add cheese and salt, pepper and mustard, stir till cheese has melted. Remove from fire.
3. Place the tomato slices on the buttered toast.
4. Place a slice of boiled egg on the tomatoes. Put under a moderate grill to heat. Pour the hot cheese sauce and serve at once.

SAUSAGES IN JACKETS

Serves 4

4 large sausages
4 slices of bread - crusts removed
50 gms of butter - melted, 1 tsp mustard paste
sweet mango or lime pickle or chutney
½ tsp pepper or red chilli powder - to taste

1. Fry the sausages and drain on paper.
2. Spread each slice of bread with mustard, then with the pickle and sprinkle red chilli powder.
3. Place a sausage across one corner of each slice of bread & roll up or fold from both sides by placing the sausage in the centre of the bread.
4. Secure with a tooth pick.
5. Brush the bread with melted butter & grill until the bread jackets are toasted and turn golden brown.

Egg Quickie

Serves 6

2-3 hard boiled eggs - mashed well
¼ cup mayonnaise
1 small onion - finely chopped
1 capsicum - finely chopped
· 1 carrot - grated
1 spring onion - finely chopped
1 tbsp mint leaves - chopped (keep few for garnish)
¼ cup cream or malai
6 slices of brown or white bread - buttered
salt, pepper

1. Mix egg, mayonnaise, onion, capsicum, carrot, spring onion, mint and cream till blended.
2. Spread the mixture on 3 slices of bread and sandwich with the remaining 3 slices. Cut into any desired shape and garnish with mint leaves.

Fried Cheese Sandwich

<u>Serves 8</u>

8 slices bread
2 eggs
½ cup milk
salt, pepper to taste
4 cheese slices
1 tomato - slices
1-2 green chillies - deseeded & cut finely
50 gm butter
oil for frying

1. Beat eggs, milk, salt and pepper together to make a batter.
2. Make sandwiches with bread, butter, cheese and tomato slices. Sprinkle green chillies.
3. Cut the sandwich into two. Dip in milk-egg batter and shallow fry in a non stick pan.

Cheese & Bacon Rolls

<u>Serves 4</u>

4 slices bacon - cut into half
4 slices of bread - cut into half
2-3 cheese cubes - cut lengthways into 8 slices
1 capsicum - cut into strips
1 tsp mustard paste

1. Roll bread slices with a rolling pin (belan) to make the slices thinner.
2. Spread with butter and the with mustard paste.
3. Place 1-2 pieces of cheese on the **unbuttered** side, top with strips of capsicum and roll up.
4. Wrap bacon around and secure with toothpicks.
5. Grill turning frequently until bacon is cooked.

Tricoloured Sandwich

Serves 4-6

8 slices bread - lightly buttered

CHICKEN FILLING
250 gms minced chicken - boneless
2 onion - chopped finely
1 tsp ginger- garlic paste
2 tomatoes - chopped finely
¼ tsp chilli powder
¼ tsp dhania powder
2 tbsp oil
½ tsp salt

POTATO FILLING
3 potatoes - boiled, peeled and mashed
¼ tsp mustard powder

¼ tsp pepper powder
½ tsp salt or to taste

CHUTNEY FILLING
½ bunch mint leaves - chopped
½ cup coriander leaves - chopped
1 onion - sliced
2 green chillies - cut finely
1 tsp lemon juice
½ tsp salt
½ tsp sugar

TOPPING
1 cup cream cheese (hang 2½ cups fresh thick curd prepared from full cream milk for 1 hour)
salt & pepper to taste

1. Heat oil in a pan and fry onion, ginger and garlic lightly.
2. Add tomatoes, chilli powder and coriander powder. Fry well.
3. Add minced chicken and salt along with ½ cup water. Cook till dry and chicken is done. Keep aside.
4. Mix potatoes with salt, pepper and mustard powder to taste.
5. Grind the chutney to a smooth paste.
6. Place a layer of mince filling on a lightly buttered slice of bread.
7. Cover with another slice. Spread the potato filling on the second slice and cover with a third slice.
8. Spread a thin layer of chutney and cover with the fourth slice.
9. Whip cream cheese with salt, pepper and a pinch of sugar. Top the loaf with it. Refrigerate for 1-2 hours.
10. Repeat with the other 4 slices.
11. Cut longitudinally and serve as a meat with soup and salad.

Basic Recipes
Thousand Island Dressing

Add a little tomato ketchup to mayonnaise given on page 94-95. Some finely chopped capsicum and onion dipped in a little vinegar and later removed from it, may also be added to the mayonnaise and tomato ketchup mixture.

Mint (Poodina) Chutney

½ cup mint (poodina) leaves (½ bunch)
1 cup hara dhania (coriander) chopped along with stem
2 green chillies
1 onion - sliced
1 tsp amchoor (dried mango pd.)
1 tsp sugar
½ tsp salt

1. Wash coriander and mint leaves.
2. Grind all ingredients together to a paste.

WHITE SAUCE

Serving ½ cup

1 tbsp butter
1 tbsp flour (maida)
½ cup cold milk
salt, pepper to taste
2 tbsp cheese - grated (optional)

1. Heat butter in a small heavy bottomed pan.
2. Add flour. Reduce flame and stir for a minute.
3. Add milk, stirring continuously. Boil. Cook till thick.
4. Add salt and pepper to taste. Add cheese.
5. Remove from fire.

MAYONNAISE (with egg)

<u>Serving 1 cup</u>

1 egg
1 cup refined oil
2 tsp lemon juice
½ tsp salt, ½ tsp powdered sugar
¼ tsp each pepper & mustard powder

1. Put egg, lemon juice, mustard powder, salt, sugar & pepper in a mixer.
2. Add the oil gradually, 1 tbsp at a time, churning the mixer at maximum speed.
3. After adding 3-4 tbsp of oil, add larger quantities (approx. ¼ cup) at a time until the mixture is thick. Do not add any more oil, as too much oil will make the mayonnaise curdle. Churn the mixer after each addition of oil.
4. The dressing becomes thick. Store in an air tight bottle in the refrigerator.

Mayonnaise (without egg)

<u>Serving 1 cup</u>

WHITE SAUCE
2 tbsp oil, 1 tbsp flour (maida)
½ cup cold milk
salt, pepper to taste

100 gm (½ cup) cream
1 tsp lemon juice
¼ tsp salt, ½ tsp mustard powder, ¼ tsp pepper powder, 1 tsp powdered sugar

1. Heat oil in a small heavy bottomed pan. Add flour. Reduce flame and stir for a minute. Add milk, stirring continuously. Boil. Cook till thick.
2. Whip white sauce after it cools to room temperature. Add lemon juice, salt, mustard powder, pepper and sugar.
3. Gently mix in the cream. Keep in the fridge.

Nita Mehta's BEST SELLERS (Vegetarian)

Cakes & Chocolates

Breakfast Vegetarian

Desserts & Puddings

Green Vegetables

Food for Children

Low Calorie Recipes

Microwave Cookery

CHINESE Vegetarian

NAVARATRI
NO ONION NO GARLIC

Soups Salads & Starters

South Indian

Vegetarian Dishes